15-minute focus

Brief Counseling
Techniques that Work

GRIEF
PROCESSING AND RECOVERY

NATIONAL CENTER for
YOUTH ISSUES

Duplication and Copyright

NCYI titles may be purchased in bulk at special discounts for
educational, business, fundraising, or promotional use. For more
information, please email sales@ncyi.org.

NATIONAL CENTER for
YOUTH ISSUES

P.O. Box 22185
Chattanooga, TN 37422-2185
423.899.5714 • 866.318.6294
fax: 423.899.4547 • www.ncyi.org

ISBN:978-1-937870-76-8 $14.95
Library of Congress Control Number: 2020913595
© 2020 National Center for Youth Issues, Chattanooga, TN
All rights reserved.
Written by: David Opalewski
Published by National Center for Youth Issues
Starkey Printing • Chattanooga, TN, U.S.A.
September 2020

Contents

See page 74 for information about Downloadable Resources.

Introduction

Imagine this situation. You arrive at school one morning to hear that one of your students died in a car accident on the way to school. Then you find out it was a student in your first period class. You think about how friendly and outgoing she was. How she was always upbeat and involved. In a few minutes you will have to face her classmates and deliver the bad news. What will you say to them? Will you carry on with a "normal" day of lessons, communicating to your students that "life goes on"? Or, will you face this difficulty by demonstrating honesty and compassion for both the deceased student and her classmates? If you have experienced such a crisis, you know just how painful this can be.

Perhaps the most valuable response to crisis is the ability to make ourselves do the things we have to do when they ought to be done, whether we like it or not. The death of a student or staff member can devastate a school and its surrounding community. When such a tragedy touches a school community, it is a school family issue, not just a counseling department issue.

Research and my experience prove that the number one need of the students and staff at this time is comfort. Shortly after the incident, shock, fear, and anxiety usually set in. People must come to normalization before quality cognitive processes can take place. Counseling is a cognitive process. If normalization does not first happen, the people being counseled cannot "connect the dots."

Research by The National Institute of Trauma and Loss in Children suggests that comfort brings normalization, thus, I developed the motto "comfort before counseling" as a best practice.[1] In an informal survey Dr. Joel Robertson and I conducted in 1994, surveying thousands of students in several states, we found that 79 percent of students wish to be comforted by their classroom teacher after a tragedy touches a school community.[2] The primary reasoning on their part is that they see their teacher every day at school and have an established relationship with that teacher. Students, for the most part, only occasionally speak with the school counselor. An overwhelming 86 percent of students also stated that they would rather not speak with a stranger about a painful event such as an unexpected school tragedy. Thus, the practice of bringing in counselors unfamiliar to students is not as effective a practice as it may seem. These outside counselors do not have relationships with the students and are only around for a day or two. When they leave the school, it is assumed the school environment is "back to normal." I am not asking classroom teachers to be counselors. I am asking them to be comforters so school counselors are in a better position to do the job of counseling.

At a conference a few years back, I met a married couple who had a first grader and kindergartener who were both students at Newtown when the terrible tragedy occurred there. Their first grader was killed, and their kindergartener survived the shooting. They shared with me that there was an outpouring of support from mental health professionals and organizations around the country. One group, in particular, came from Chicago and, in this family's opinion, made the most positive impact on the students and staff who survived the tragedy. But they weren't people. They were golden retrievers. As you know, golden retrievers can't talk. Yet, this couple said that their kindergartener told the dogs things that he wouldn't share with the mental health professionals. What made these dogs so helpful? I believe it was their non-judgmental presence. That is more powerful than anything anyone can say. Your presence at these difficult times shows that you care.

***

In my thirty-three years in K–12 education, I experienced the deaths of twenty-six students and staff members combined. Some of my experiences were as follows:

- I became a replacement teacher in a fifth-grade classroom for a teacher who was killed in an accident in the middle of the school year.
- An eighth-grade boy was hit and killed while riding his bike to school.
- An eighth-grade girl was killed after crashing into a garbage truck while riding a four-wheeler.
- A senior in high school unexpectantly died by suicide one morning before school.
- A popular industrial arts teacher died suddenly from a heart attack before school.
- A seventh-grade girl died of a brain aneurism during the school day outside my classroom.

None of us can fully prepare for tragedies such as these. Even with the best preparation, our feet are still knocked out from under us when it happens. The loss of a student or staff member impacts the entire school family. It is shocking and heartbreaking. It impacts students every time they walk into a classroom and see an empty desk, a space that reminds them of the person who died, or a substitute teacher sitting in for a teacher who died.

In this short book, I wish to share with you the lessons I have learned in order to help you, your students, the parents of your students, and your staff through these challenging times.

1 Lessons Learned in Loss

One of the most important lessons I learned in dealing with loss in the education setting was that the comforting phase must come before counseling takes place. This phase is best accomplished in what I call Classroom Defusing Discussions facilitated by the teacher. I will provide an example in just a moment, but first I want to share some basic principles for the classroom defusing discussions. Teachers, educators, and counselors should all keep these principles in mind.

- Explanations must be simple, not medical or theological.
- Over-explaining reflects your own anxiety to the students.
- Students need to talk, not just be talked to!
- When talking to students about suicide, *never* say "he or she is better off."
- It is not the *expression* but the *suppression* of feeling that is most harmful.
- The way you are most doomed to failure in handling a tragedy is to deny or ignore it.
- Students' greatest needs at this time are *trust* and *truth*.

Classroom Defusing Discussion

1. The classroom teacher should start with an opening statement:

We are sad to learn that _____ in the _____ grade died last night as a result of a car accident. This is all the information we have at this time. As more information becomes available, such as funeral arrangements and memorial services, we will pass it on to you. After our discussion here, counselors will be available in a support room should anyone like to talk further about feelings you are experiencing.

2. Allow a minute or two for the news to sink in for students.

3. The teacher then should express how he/she is impacted by the incident. This is very important as the students at this time especially need to see the teacher as a person, not as a teacher. "I am very sad and shocked by this news, and I am especially sad for _____'s family."

4. Ask students to share positive memories of the deceased.

5. Talk about feelings of grief. (See Appendix 2: Normal Versus Abnormal Grief.)

6. Encourage students to attend the visitation and funeral, and inform them of what to expect at the funeral home and funeral in regards to the family's religion and culture. You may ask, "How many of you have been to a visitation or funeral before? They can be very sad, and you might see some people crying. It may be quiet and very solemn. But attending a funeral is a way we can show that we care and give our respect to a family in their time of loss. It may feel a little awkward or scary at first. But it means a lot to a family to hear what their loved ones meant to others. Be aware that you may see customs you haven't seen before and don't understand, but that is okay."

7. Encourage students to make a card, draw a picture, plan a memorial at the school, etc.

8. Tell the students that the class is going to move on to classroom work, but tell them that they can stop working at any point to further discuss the tragedy or if they are simply feeling overwhelmed by grief.

9. Students who opt to go to the counseling room should be accompanied by an adult both there and returning to the classroom.

10. Station both female and male staff members in the hallways to assist staff if needed. Students may wish to go to the restroom to cry or dry their faces and should be allowed to do so.

11. Tell young children that they can bring a stuffed animal or something familiar with them to school to provide security.

Important Points

The teacher must have all the facts about the incident from the school crisis team to dispel any rumors. These rumors can make a sad situation much worse. If possible, the teacher should also have time to personally process the tragedy in an information/debriefing session with colleagues. If we as adults don't tend to our feelings in these situations, how can we care for and comfort our students?

During this session, the staff should discuss questions the students may bring up, such as:

1. Why did the death happen?
2. What is a funeral and what happens at a funeral?
3. Will others I love die?
4. What will happen to me if one of my parents or both of my parents die?

There are no easy answers to these questions. However, the staff discussion session can create consistency in how to respond to students. Getting advice from the school counselor is very important during the session.

The other day, I was on an airplane traveling to a conference. Before takeoff, the flight attendant went through the safety procedures in case a crisis occurred during flight. If you've ever flown, you know that one of the procedures is that oxygen masks will come down from the ceiling if at any point the cabin loses air pressure. The instruction is to *put on your own mask before you assist anyone else with theirs*. It struck me that the same should occur in a school crisis situation. Whenever possible, school staff should be given the opportunity to put on their own oxygen masks first. This could be accomplished by scheduling a meeting with administration and teachers, giving them time to process what has happened so they are better prepared to communicate with their students.

Things We Shouldn't Say

It's also important to note that there are actually things we should never say to students after the loss of a loved one. Although most people know this already, you'd be surprised what even the most self-aware person will say when they don't know what else to say. Even when our words are well-intentioned, they can often make a heartbreaking situation much worse. Here are a few examples of things we shouldn't say:

- "She wouldn't want you to be sad." — Since the child is sad, saying this may make them feel like they are disappointing their deceased friend.
- "This will make you stronger." — Saying this implies that they are weak.
- "He is in a better place." — This can be confusing and hurtful because the child or adolescent wants the person to be with them.
- "I know how you feel." — This communicates that you don't need to hear what the student has to say.
- "God needed your friend." — Saying this implies that they didn't need her enough.

I personally witnessed one of the above statements when I was working in a funeral home during graduate school. While writing my master's degree thesis, *Death Education: Guidelines for Classroom Teachers*, I worked part time in a funeral home as the aftercare consultant to the families of the deceased.

In one particular situation, I was helping during a visitation for a man who left behind a wife and an eleven-year-old son. As I stood in the hallway outside the chapel listening to the boy talk about his father, a lady (later found out to be his aunt) came up to him and said, "Don't worry, Thomas. God needed your dad." After she walked away, Thomas (not his real name) looked up at me and said, "I guess I didn't need my dad enough." My heart broke for Thomas as I saw the horrible look of guilt wash over his face.

Statements like this send the often unintentional but extremely hurtful message: "Stop feeling so bad." It is impossible to tell anyone how to feel. These statements minimize and ignore the feelings of the grieving person who has been touched by a death. There are many ways we can minimize someone's feelings, but the biggest piece of advice I can give on this hurtful approach is this: when speaking to a grieving person, never start a sentence with "at least." "At least they don't have to suffer anymore." "At least they are in a better place." "At least you still have the rest of your family." None of these statements are helpful.

Finding the Right Words

The following is adapted from the December 2010 issue of *Good Housekeeping* magazine that listed "not helpful" and "more helpful" things to say to someone who is going through a difficult time:[3]

NOT HELPFUL	MORE HELPFUL
I know how you feel.	I can only imagine how hard this must be.
I know what that's like.	Do you mind telling me what it's like?
It's time to put this behind you.	This might take time.
It could be worse.	You have a lot on your plate.
Keep the faith.	I'm thinking of you every day.
It happened for the best.	I'm so sorry this happened.

This list could be endless. The lesson is to stop and imagine what the child needs to hear from you, not what you feel you "need" to say. We cannot and should not try to fix the tragedy. Although we wish these things would never happen, when properly handled, the incident can become a growth experience instead of just a tragic experience.

One example of a growth experience happened when I was the family liaison on our school crisis team. One morning an eighth-grade boy was killed riding his bike to school. Shortly after the incident, I met with his parents to express my condolences, share my warm feelings for their son, and make a list of immediate needs we as their school family could help them with. Our staff provided meals, picked up relatives at the airport and bus station, arranged house-sitting for them during the visitation and funeral service, and helped with many other needs.

The deceased boy's classmates must have been observing the ways we were serving his family. On the morning of the funeral, four inches of new snow fell to the ground. Without any requests from our staff, four eighth-grade boys showed up at the family's house and shoveled the sidewalk and driveway because they wanted to help the family as well. This wasn't just a growth experience for our school staff. This was a growth experience for these students too. They followed our example and reached out to help this family in their time of need.

In Conclusion

When loss happens in our school community, what we say as teachers and educators is extremely important. We should provide a familiar place of comfort for our students. We should be consistent, but not too lax or too rigid. We should maintain the same boundaries and rules but allow for students to talk or ask questions when they need to. At the same time, we should give the student the right not to share if they don't want to. We all react to tragedy differently, and we all move at different speeds through the grief process. We can't expect a child or adolescent to feel something they do not. And we should speak with understanding, avoiding unhelpful words and replacing them with words of empathy. Finally, if you need additional help or see students who are stuffing their emotions, speak to the school counselor and ask for guidance.

A Student's Story

Helen (not her real name) was a seventh-grade student of mine whose father died of a sudden heart attack. Helen's father, Steve (also not his real name), and I had once worked on a school fundraiser together and became good friends. At his funeral, I did not get the chance to talk to Helen. When she came back to school a week after the funeral, I greeted her and said, "Helen, I am sorry about you losing your father. I got to know him well during our school fundraiser and really enjoyed working with him. He became a valued friend of mine, and I will miss him."

About a month later, on the last day of school, the students were dismissed and the hallways were empty. As I walked back to my classroom from being on hall duty, Helen was waiting to talk to me. She said, "Mr. Opalewski, I want to thank you for what you said to me the day I came back to school after my dad's funeral." I asked her, "Didn't your other teachers say something to you?" "Yes," she responded. "They all told me they were sorry, but you said my dad's name. Thank you."

In that moment, I remembered that one of the greatest fears of children and adolescents after losing a loved one is that they are going to be forgotten. When you mention the name of their deceased loved one, you assure them that they will not be forgotten and you communicate that you are willing to take the time to be available if they should need to talk to you.

QUESTIONS to CONSIDER

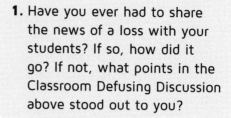

1. Have you ever had to share the news of a loss with your students? If so, how did it go? If not, what points in the Classroom Defusing Discussion above stood out to you?

2. What are some things we should never say to students when talking about death or suicide?

3. What are some of the more helpful things we should say to students when addressing loss?

KEY POINTS

- When dealing with loss in the classroom setting, comforting should always come before counseling.

- In the Classroom Defusing Discussion, teachers should communicate the loss to their students with empathy and without over-explaining. They should give the students time to talk and share, explain funeral arrangements and what to expect, and give them the opportunity to visit the counseling room.

- Even the most well-intentioned people can say hurtful things to someone who has experienced loss. It is important to know the things we should *never* say and to learn the more helpful things to say instead.

2 Basic Grief Facts for Children

Grief is a unique journey. It is proven that no two people grieve in the same way. It is a foreign emotion, and if it doesn't get addressed, it goes underground—or it becomes suppressed. Once it goes underground, it will eventually resurface and most likely will be more damaging than it originally was at the start. Grief is a normal response to loss, and we must let people walk through it in their own way. We also can't try to take away a person's pain; rather, we should let the grieving person feel their pain.

When I was a boy, I got a new bike for Christmas. A few days later, while riding, I lost control and fell off and scraped my elbow. I did not want my mother to clean it and put antiseptic on because I knew it would hurt. My mother, however, knew that cleaning my wound, no matter how much it hurt, would help it heal. If I had refused to have the wound cleaned because it hurt to do so, an infection could have set in and my problem—and pain—would have become much worse. Thus, we have the analogy for grief: If we don't feel our pain, we won't heal. I had to feel the pain of the cleaning in order for my wound to heal.

When dealing with grief, it is important to know the difference between suffering and pain. Suffering might look like having anxiety attacks about what might happen next as a result of the pain, which makes the pain more intense. "What is it going to be like not having my dad?" "What is going to happen to Mom now that Dad is not going to be around?" "Will we have to move and I change schools?" Suffering also can manifest in physical maladies such as increased sickness, as we know the immune system is impacted. It also can materialize in a deep feeling of loneliness. We can't fix the pain others feel, but we can attend to it by reducing the things (suffering) that make the pain worse or by looking for ways that might help make the situation just a little bit better. There is no formula to help in every situation, but there are some general guidelines for helping someone navigate grief.

Specifics Regarding Grieving Children

A child who experiences the death of a parent, sibling, or other close loved one does indeed grieve. These grieving children must have the loving guidance of an adult if they are to navigate the grieving process and grow to be emotionally healthy. As you can imagine, young children generally face more challenges than adults in understanding and grieving a loss. They do not have the benefit of life experiences and emotional maturity that adults have when facing these life-changing challenges. In addition to feeling sad, children may feel shock, anger, confusion, guilt, fear, and insecurity. All of these emotions can feel overwhelming to children, and they look to adults to help them make sense of what they are experiencing.

Before Discussing the Sudden Death of a Classmate

The following is a list of suggestions for teachers or other adults to consider before discussing the sudden death of a classmate.

1. Stop. Breathe. Calm yourself.
2. Get in touch with your own feelings.
3. Think about what you want to say beforehand.

4. Use short sentences and age-appropriate vocabulary.

5. Do not promise anything you can't deliver.

6. Encourage the expression of all feelings.

7. Listen to students' questions.

8. Remember, grief is a process. It is not limited by time.

9. Don't anticipate an "appropriate" response from students. They are not adults.

10. Young children seem to be more attentive sitting on the floor or in a circle with you sitting with them. Proximity is important!

Explaining the Sudden Death of a Classmate

The sudden death of another child, a friend, or a classmate can be very scary for a child. It introduces a profound sense of vulnerability into their world, making them realize that something painful and scary can happen to someone their age. In discussing these situations with a child or group of children, the following points are important to keep in mind:

1. When discussing death with children, you must communicate that you don't have all the answers. If a child asks a question that you don't know the answer to, simply reply "I don't know." This communicates a sense of honesty and a willingness to be on the child's level.

2. Clearly stress that what has happened is rare and that it hardly ever happens. When children get sick, they get well. When children get out of their parent's car and walk across the street to school, they do it safely. That is why when a tragedy like this happens, everybody is so shocked and sad. Something that shouldn't have happened did happen, and it is hard for everyone to come to terms with it.

3. Let students know that what happened to Susie was not a punishment for her being bad. Say, "If you are remembering

that Susie did something a little naughty a few days ago, then yesterday she became suddenly sick and died, that doesn't mean that if you do the same thing, something bad is going to happen to you. Susie didn't get sick because she was a bad girl and deserved to get sick. She deserved to live, play, and have fun. This terrible, unexplainable thing just happened."

4. Do not try to "fix" the problem. In caring for and comforting children during their grief, it should be our objective to help them grow in their own coping skills, not give them ours.

What Adults Should Not Tell Grieving Children About Death

1. Don't say, "Max suffered from cancer and is no longer in pain. He is in a better place." The "better place" can be confusing to young children.

2. Don't say, "Your dad has gone on a long journey." Vague explanations are not healthy for children who are processing grief. They may think he is coming back.

3. Don't say, "Our friend Samuel is sleeping now." There is a major difference between sleep and death, and telling children something that is untrue may cause unnecessary anxiety.

4. Don't say, "Your mom is the lucky one. She's in heaven now." Pushing your theological beliefs on the child can cause more pain for an angry, grieving child.

5. Don't say, "You have to be the man of the house and take care of your mother and sister now." This puts additional burdens and expectations on the child.

6. Don't answer a child's questions about death with stories or fairy tales. This will only add to their confusion.

Special Considerations – Ages Six to Nine

Although children between the ages of six and nine are starting to have an understanding of death, the permanence of death is still hard to comprehend. They may feel that death is something that happens to others, not them. Some may believe the person who died is alive in the ground. Because they may not have the vocabulary to express verbally how they are feeling, they may express it in their behavior. Also, their questions may revolve around the decomposition of the body and the biological process of death. They may also ask a question you don't have an answer for. Your response should be "I don't know." Then you may consider following up by saying, "Are you surprised that I don't know everything about death? Please don't be. We can still talk about it. You can learn from me and I can learn from you. We can help each other."

Special Considerations – Ages Nine to Twelve

At this age, children are developing a better understanding of death. They are ready for more information such as why the death happened, information and reason for funerals, whether or not another loved one might die, and who will take care of them if their parents or guardian dies. Once again, honesty is very important in responding to the child's questions and concerns. Your honesty communicates your willingness to get to the child's level of understanding. Children at this age can ask a plethora of diverse questions. In past experience, I have found it difficult to categorize common questions and concerns asked by this age group. I have learned, however, that my presence is more important than anything I can say. If you feel you have to say something, statements such as "I care about you," "You were a wonderful brother to your sister," "Your sister loved you," and "You are a wonderful son," may be helpful. What you have in your heart is far more important than what you have in your head. In the child's mind, knowing that you care is more important than what you know.

Common Myths Concerning Children and Grief

There are many myths surrounding children and grief, but some of the most common myths are listed below. My intention is to clear up any possible misconceptions about the grief process of children. Please keep in mind this is a list of common myths rather than an exhaustive list.

1. *A child's grief is a much shorter duration than an adult's grief.*

   In my experience as a counselor and grief support group facilitator, I have worked with middle, high school, and college students (as well as adults in my aftercare support group) who were still working through grief incidents from childhood. We can't put a timetable on grief. There is no evidence that children grieve for shorter periods than adults, and this is simply not the way grief works. We can experience grief from one incident in childhood throughout different stages of our lives.

2. *There is a predictable and orderly stage-like progression to a child's grief experiences.*

   Grief is a unique and foreign experience to all people, regardless of age. Factors such as temperament, past trauma experiences, parenting styles, loss of a sibling, and so on, all have an influence on an individual's grief process.

3. *Children are not affected by the grief of the adults around them.*

   A surviving parent's inability to mourn has proven to be a major hindrance to a child's grief process. In fact, it does not allow the child to mourn. The inability of the parents to grieve the loss of a family member creates an insecure environment for the child and contributes to the child's confusion about the death and their part in it.

4. *The trauma of childhood grief always leads to a maladjusted life.*

   Children are more resilient than most adults give them credit for. Although we can't ever get over the grief of a loved one, we can get through it and heal. "Getting over the grief" implies that there will come a day when we don't care anymore. But we will always care. Countless people who have suffered a death of a loved one during childhood don't move on; *they move forward* with the care of many like you. Many of these people have developed an appreciation for life and are frontline comforters to people who are working through a grief process.

5. *Children who cry are being weak and harming themselves.*

   Crying is a healthy method of expressing and releasing pent-up emotions. Recently, it has been discovered that the brain of a person (including children) who has suffered a loss produces an excess amount of the chemical cortisol. A surplus of cortisol interferes with the executive functioning of the brain by burning serotonin, which is the relaxing chemical of the brain. Researchers recently found large amounts of cortisol in the tears of grieving people.[4] Crying is healthy in the fact that it is one way to release excess cortisol. In his book *Good Grief*, Granger Westberg says, "Tears are God's tranquilizers; use them!"[5]

6. *The goal in helping grieving children is to "get them over" their grief.*

   The goal should never be for children to get over their grief, but to get through it, heal, and move forward. We can help them do this by remembering the good times they have had with their loved one and reassuring them that they will not be forgotten.

Grieving Children Risk Factors

By failing to comfort and attend to children grieving the death of a loved one, friend, or classmate, we are exposing them to the following risk factors:

1. Depression lasting into adulthood
2. Anxiety disorders
3. Increased illness
4. Poor school performance
5. Significantly lower levels of self-esteem
6. Greater feelings of loss of control – "I am a victim"
7. Regressive behavior – acting out behaviors
8. Clinical depression

Ways to Help

The best advice I can give teachers, educators, and counselors is to be compassionately honest. Children know when you are not being honest with them. I have *never* had a child or adolescent say to me "I am glad I was lied to." So, start with honesty, and build on this key piece of advice.

In addition to being honest, here are some other ways you can help children navigate loss:

1. Allow and encourage creative ways to remember the deceased person. Make a collage of the deceased using pictures of them participating in school or social activities with fellow friends and classmates, collect money to contribute to a local charity, organize a memorial service for the school, etc.

2. Be their companion in the conversation. Ask questions like: "What was Billy like?" and "What are some good memories you have of him?"

3. Mirror what children tell you in their words. When they say, "I am very sad," repeat, "Yes, I am also very sad."

4. Stay away from "why" statements, since these can be seen or perceived as interrogating. For example, instead of asking, "Why did you feel hurt when your friends seem to ignore you?" ask, "How are your friends acting differently than before the death?"

5. Refrain from asking questions that evoke a yes or no answer. For example, instead of asking, "Was it hard coming back to school?" a better question is "What does it feel like coming back to school?"

6. Just be present. Your presence speaks louder than any words you can say.

7. Listen, Listen, Listen. As the old nursery rhyme says,

   A wise old owl lived in an oak.
   The more he saw the less he spoke.
   The less he spoke the more he heard.
   Why can't we all be like that wise old bird?

8. Finally, remember, when we start to fix, we begin to fail.

Classroom Activities for Dealing with Grief

One of the most innate things students will want to do is create something to express and work through their grief. Here is a short list of possible classroom activities you can do with your students:

1. Write individual sympathy letters or a class sympathy letter to the family of the deceased.

2. Give students time to do an art project honoring the deceased.

3. Make a "treasure box" memorial for the family. You can include letters, poems, artwork, or anything that helps the family remember their loved one. (Have an adult oversee this project to make sure everything is appropriate.)

4. Make a pictorial poster board for display at the funeral home visitation, school common area, or other appropriate and meaningful place.

5. Create a T-shirt with the deceased person's silhouette on the front, and on the back print something like "*Thank You for Touching So Many Lives.*" Sell the T-shirts and contribute the proceeds to a local charity designated by the family. This works well for a deceased staff member. Just make sure you place an adult in charge of the process, from the T-shirt sales to the charitable contribution.

Helping Parents Help Their Child

A child growing up in today's world is all too aware of the reality of death, perhaps more than parents realize. Of course, they experience death in TV shows and movies, many have grandparents, family members, or pets who die, and there is the vivid reality of the internet or video games.

Helping children deal with death is the responsibility of every parent whose child is grieving. Even when the child is seeing a counselor, the parent still has the important role of comforting and reassuring the child. Helping children deal with death is especially challenging when the parent is also grieving the loss. In this case, perhaps the most important thing the parent can do is find appropriate ways to deal with their own grief.

Below is a list of suggestions to share with parents who need help talking about death with their children:

• Encourage your child to tell you how they feel about the death, what they think, and what they know.

- Attempt to answer your child's questions in the spirit they were asked.

- Don't communicate to your child—either in words or actions—that they must accept your answer or explanation of what happened. "It is okay if you don't see things exactly the way I do."

- Keep your voice calm when talking with your child. Research shows we have a 75 percent greater chance of having a successful conversation if we keep our voice calm.[6]

- Be present. Your presence if far more important than having all the answers.

- Be honest. Children know when you are not being honest with them. If you don't know the answer to a question, look them in the eyes and say, "I don't know."

- Give your child the right not to share if they don't want to. However, let them know that when they are ready to share, you will be ready to listen.

- Listen! Your child needs to talk more than being talked to.

Question from Parents: Should My Child Attend the Funeral Service?

I suggest parents use their best judgment in this decision. Please consider that, at a young age, children are interested in events such as birthdays, weddings, and other forms of celebration. Denying your child the opportunity to attend this important family event may very well cause fear and may even interfere in their emotional resolution of the death. However, it is important for parents to prepare children for what they will see and possibly experience at the funeral. Prepare them by saying, "You may see people crying and you may see people laughing. It may be very quiet, or you may see people talking very loudly. It is all okay."

In Conclusion

In his book *Healing the Bereaved Child*, Dr. Alan Wolfelt makes a profound statement: "Any child old enough to love is old enough to grieve."[7] In my life, I have found this statement to be true. I am married to a former widow who had a twenty-one-month-old son and was two months pregnant with another boy when the sudden death of her husband occurred. We met and started dating four years later, and she shared with me how both boys, including the one in the womb, grieved the loss of their father. As we continued on in our courtship and into our married life, I clearly saw that her statement was true. The excuse that "they are too young to grieve" is just an excuse not to deal with this difficult situation. We shouldn't try to protect our children from such realities of life because, unfortunately, incidents do occur and we need to help them cope and give them hope.

Our main objective should be to bring hope to a young child who is confused, scared, and sad. As a parent of three children (I adopted my wife's first two sons), I often found myself helping them deal with these feelings. As I look back on those times, I realize the vast importance of this parental/adult role. Many adults think that death issues are too complicated for children to understand, but I wholly disagree! We can talk to children about death and provide a listening ear for all their thoughts and feelings.

A Student's Story

A few years ago, at a grief conference, I heard a story of a young female child who asked the question: "How long is death?" The adult answered, "Death is permanent." The young girl then said, "Oh, that is not so bad. My mother has permanents at the hairdresser. It doesn't last so long." The point here is that children need simple and honest, age-appropriate explanations about death. Before answering, the adult should have considered the reason the child asked the question. The reason being, at this time, the child was missing a loved one who had passed away. Because the adult failed to consider the reason for the child's question, and offer an age-appropriate response, the answer was misleading and did not meet the need of the child. It is critical that we start with listening to the child and considering their needs before we offer any sort of explanations about death.

QUESTIONS to CONSIDER

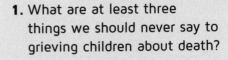

1. What are at least three things we should never say to grieving children about death?

2. What are some clear risk factors for grieving children?

3. Have you ever experienced a loss at your school? If so, how have you helped the students navigate the loss? If not, which of the listed activities in this chapter do you think would help your students work through their grief?

KEY POINTS

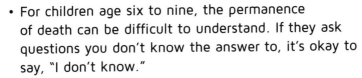

- Young children do grieve and need the loving guidance of adults to navigate loss.

- For children age six to nine, the permanence of death can be difficult to understand. If they ask questions you don't know the answer to, it's okay to say, "I don't know."

- For children age nine to twelve, they have a much better understanding of death, so honesty is incredibly important when speaking to them. Also, your presence is more important than anything you can say.

- There are many myths surrounding the grief process for children. Some important things to note are that children can grieve just as long as the adults around them, children are affected by the grieving adults around them, and rather than helping children get over their grief, we should help them through it.

3 Basic Grief Facts for Adolescents

Adolescents are a unique set of grievers with unique challenges. They are not children and not adults, yet most of the time they are treated as one or the other. Adolescent grief is an area in need of much more research. The information I share in this chapter comes from my experience facilitating adolescent grief support groups. I hope that what I learned from this growing and maturing group of students can help you as you interact with them and help them navigate loss and grief.

Adolescent Grief Facts

Most deaths that adolescents experience are sudden or untimely deaths. Many students will react with feelings of disbelief and numbness. Their survival mechanisms tell them they must push others away to survive. Rage fantasies are more common in this age group than any other. This is their way of saying, "I protest this death." Sometimes these rage factors include a desire to inflict harm on the person responsible for the incident (for example: a drunk driver causing the death of a friend). Most adolescents know not to act on these feelings. If these feelings surface, most often an adult can talk them down and help them see that this is their anger speaking.

The death of a parent is especially difficult for adolescents. Most often, the family dynamics change dramatically causing insecurities in these students. Also, based upon my observations from working for three years as an aftercare consultant for a funeral home, adolescents are extremely close to boyfriends, girlfriends, and best friends. Many times, their grief is overlooked because society tends to focus on the "primary" grievers—the deceased person's immediate family.

Grieving Adolescents in School

After a tragedy affecting the school family, adolescent students should not be asked to continue with schoolwork as if nothing happened. The work of grieving must take precedence if these students are to begin the healing process. Teachers need to understand this temporary shift in priorities and give students the time they need to talk about the tragedy with teachers and each other. Also, important events like prom or graduation are usually difficult times for students who have lost a classmate, not only after a short time, but also years later. Students can honor classmates who have died by creating "In Memory" slides or photos for important events to remember their friends.

What Not to Do

When addressing the incident with students, it is important to refrain from the following actions. Do not . . .

1. Be judgmental, criticize, or blame – "If he wasn't drinking and driving, he would be alive." Students most likely already know this, so calling it out is not helpful. They need comfort at this time, and this doesn't bring comfort. It also doesn't show empathy.

2. Do most of the talking. Students need to talk more than they are talked to.

3. Tell half-truths. "She died from a sudden illness," when actually she took her own life. Eventually, they will learn the truth and you will lose their trust.

4. Minimize the loss. "At least he didn't suffer." "At least you have a brother you can talk to." Or "He is in a better place."

5. Use clichés such as "We all will die sometime" or "We never know when it's our turn to die."

6. Say "I know how you feel."

7. Expect them to think like an adult.

8. Assume that a student's busy activity means they are being disrespectful or disinterested. Chances are this is most likely a survival tactic for them.

9. Tell students how they should feel.

What to Do

There are plenty of ways we can help adolescents feel heard and understood in times of tragedy and loss. Here are some helpful things you can do to show empathy and understanding for your students.

1. Allow the loss to take precedence with classmates. They need to talk with each other about the loss at this age much more so than they did when they were younger.

2. Trust your instincts for knowing the right thing to do and say. There is no perfect script. When your heart is right about wanting to help, in my opinion, most of the things you do and say will be right.

3. Initiate the discussion of the loss. Students will be more likely to open up if you show that you are struggling with the news as well.

4. Encourage students to attend the visitation, funeral, or memorial service. Also, give them information about what to expect for different religions, cultures, and so on.

5. Give students an opportunity to do something constructive for the deceased's family. You might write individual letters or create a box that holds slips of paper with students' favorite memories of their classmate.

6. Communicate the knowledge that all feelings are okay and need to be appropriately expressed.

7. Marshal positive forces in the students' lives. Point to the fact that life is also filled with many good things. Your main objectives are to comfort and bring hope without minimizing the tragedy. Don't start a sentence using the words "at least."

Death of a Sibling

The death of a sibling during childhood or adolescence comes at a critical time in their emotional and social development. Whether the relationship was close or strained, the loss is grieved. During my thirty-plus years of working with families who lost a loved one, I have learned that when death impacts a family, everyone has a high need to be understood, and a natural incapacity to be understanding. The family unit is most likely to be stressed and distanced during this immediate time of grief. Research from Catholic and Lutheran Family Services says that "about 40 percent of marriages will end in divorce within two years after the death of a child."[8] This is a time when adolescents need adults to give them encouragement and hope. It is common for adolescents to feel they are losing their sense of self, and they need their parents' presence, especially during this difficult time. Additionally, the grieving sibling needs to be reminded that their parents are grieving, too.

General Ways of Coping

Adolescents find a myriad of ways to cope with the loss of a sibling. There are so many factors that play into how and why they cope the way they do—from family dynamics, to pressure from others, to feeling that their identity has shifted.

Cloning

It is common for grieving adolescents to try to become like a clone of their deceased sibling. They hear so much praise from others about their brother or sister that they then attempt to become that "perfect" person. In doing so, they lose a sense of who they are. My advice to adults working with these grieving students is to tell them, "This situation is no longer about your deceased sibling, but about you and your survival." With all the praise heaped on the deceased sibling, many adolescents begin to believe that they don't matter. They may no longer recognize their unique identity, which leads them to feeling lost.

Overachieving

Many adolescents are at the age where they can recognize the pain on their parents' faces. They want their parents to be happy again; therefore, they may attempt to overachieve academically or in extracurricular activities at school. They try so hard to be the perfect child for their parents, but they quickly become frustrated when they realize they can't keep up. They become stuck between helping their parents and caring for their own well-being. As the struggle progresses, resentment occurs, causing the adolescent to spiral into complex emotional issues.

Isolation

Because adolescents are being treated differently during this time by adults and peers, they don't feel like they belong anywhere in their social environment, so they separate themselves from the people who care about them most. They don't want to be seen as different, yet everything about their world does feel different. It is very difficult for them to be around people who need them to feel better when they know they can't.

Unique Issues for Adolescents

As an adolescent support group facilitator, I discovered challenges that many adolescents face that may not be unique to grieving people but are very challenging to these students.

Numbness

One common issue adolescents face is the feeling of numbness. One group of adolescents expressed that they "can't feel anything" after a friend of theirs died suddenly in a car accident. This numbness is a common occurrence for many people after the loss of someone close. What these adolescents need us to do is normalize their feelings. We should clearly communicate that when a person is emotionally overwhelmed, their mind tends to shut down the reality of what happened. This is the mind's way of protecting them from feeling overwhelmed with pain. We should stress that they don't have to feel guilty about this. (Remember, we shouldn't tell them what to feel.) We can encourage the adolescent to give it some time and let their feelings out when they are ready to come out. Finally, we can remind them that there is usually a different timetable for each person to express these feelings.

Confusion on How They Should Be Acting

As the adolescent looks around at their friends, they may see many people crying and others showing no emotion at all. We need to stress to the adolescent that grief takes many forms and there is no single way to respond to a death. Just because some people are quiet and don't talk about it doesn't mean they aren't affected by the incident. They may be tearing apart inside. There is no right or wrong way to respond, and the best thing we can do is give people space and permission to grieve in their own way.

Expressing Deep Sadness for the Death of Someone They Weren't Close To

A few years back my wife and I got a call late at night from our son who was a freshman in college. He just heard that a fellow student-athlete was killed in a car accident. He talked to us for almost two hours. He was emotionally upset. The next day, I drove to campus to have lunch with him. During this time, he expressed confusion over the degree of emotion he expressed the previous evening. His confusion was over the fact that they were on different teams and he did not know the deceased personally. "Why am I feeling so sad?" was his lament to me. Perhaps this tragedy reminded our son of his own mortality. At the same time, it showed that he has a good heart, capable of loving and caring for people.

Some adolescents I have counseled expressed deep sadness for the death of someone they weren't really that close to. As a result, they often felt that they had an emotional deficiency—as if there was something wrong with them for feeling so strongly when they didn't believe they should have. When this happens, adolescents need to be reminded that they don't have to be a person's best friend to feel the pain of grief when a person dies. As I went deeper with these adolescents, I discovered that some of them were reminded of previous losses they have experienced, and these new deaths triggered those older feelings of loss. The loss of human life is tragic, whether we knew that person closely or not. And people will respond differently to loss based on personality, past experiences, and so on.

Circle of Friends Changes

Adolescents often experience a circle of friends change following the death of one of the people in their group. This may happen a few months after the incident, when one or more people in the friend group begin isolating from each other, adding to the sadness of the loss. Some people in the group may need to break away to get a handle on their feelings. Usually this is temporary. However, teachers, counselors, and educators should encourage a circle of friends to at least check in with each other even though it may be difficult to hang out together. In time, the friendships are rekindled, and students begin hanging out with each other again.

Parents Attempting to Fix

Because of their deep love for their children, parents often struggle watching their children grieve. As a result, they may try to "fix" the situation by smothering their child or minimizing the situation. When an adolescent shares this problem with us, we can remind them of their parents' love and tell them how difficult it is for parents to watch their children suffer. We can communicate that although their parents mean well, they do have a right to their own space. We can encourage the grieving adolescent to kindly ask their parents for space to grieve. And rather than their parents telling them what to feel, students should communicate that what they need most is their parents' presence and non-judgmental listening.

How to Encourage Adolescents

There are many ways we as adults can encourage adolescents through these difficult times. It is important that we acknowledge how hard this is and how life-changing it can be. Here are some particularly helpful things we can say to students navigating loss and grief.

1. Grief is hard work. It takes energy to grieve and you will at times feel fatigued. But there are ways to do it in a healthy way.

2. You will never get over the loss and heartache of losing [your sister], but you can get through it and heal. You will always remember her, and you can find ways to honor her memory.

3. Your method of coping doesn't have to define you or change who you are.

4. You don't move on; you move forward. Moving on means you will forget your sister. Moving forward means you remember and cherish the good times you had with her,

and you can love and appreciate your family more than before.

5. Being sad about the loss of your friend or sibling means you have a good heart capable of loving others. This is a good thing.

Anticipated Death

The mistake many adults make when comforting a student dealing with an anticipated death is that they consider this situation to be a "good death." They mistakenly assume the child or teen has had the opportunity to come to terms with the situation and that somehow this makes it less painful. This mindset ignores the emotional strains and longsuffering of families dealing with a terminal illness.

Stress with a Dying Loved One

There are many strains and stresses on people who have a dying loved one. Some of these are:

1. The deterioration of the dying person—physical, emotional, mental

2. Fear of the unknown— "What will my life be like after the death?"

3. The inability to help change the situation

4. The loss of seeing the world as a safe place

5. The child's/teen's fear of the intensity of their own emotional reaction at the time of death

What Not to Do When Talking to an Adolescent Facing the Anticipated Death of a Loved One

1. Do most of the talking when meeting with the student
2. Avoid the student
3. Minimize the situation
4. Compete in the "Grief Olympics" by sharing a personal struggle. This only communicates to the student that their situation is not as bad as yours was.

Communication

As I mentioned before, when talking with a person in an emotionally charged or sad situation, the tone of our voice is extremely important. We can say the right thing, but if our tone is shrill, communication suffers. Research shows that people pay more attention to our tone of voice than anything else.[9] When it comes to difficult conversations, we must choose both our words and tone carefully.

Helping Parents Help Their Adolescents

In all my years of working with grieving adolescents, I have concluded that there is no one method that is most effective in guiding them through the grief process. One of the most important pieces of advice I stress to parents in helping their grieving kids is that *what is in their heart is more important than what is in their head*. Here are a few fundamental points for parents to keep in mind:

- Make every effort to enter your child's world and get a glimpse of their perspectives. They don't have the life experience of most adults and therefore aren't able to think like adults.

- Remember, you don't know how they feel. A better approach might be "I have had a similar loss and kind of have an idea of what you may feel."

- Don't tell them what they should be feeling. When you do this, you aren't validating their pain.

- Don't minimize their loss. Many well-meaning adults feel that minimizing the incident might help their child focus on more positive things. However, the fact is, their pain keeps them from focusing on anything but their pain.

- Communicate that we don't move on from hard losses. Moving on means we will forget, and we will never forget this loss. We can get through it and heal by remembering and appreciating the good times we had with the person who died. Healing helps us move forward.

- Grieving adolescents have taught me that their greatest fear after the death of a loved one or close friend is that the person will be forgotten. When you are speaking to your child, mention the person by name. Reassure them that this person won't be forgotten, and this will help **lessen** their fear.

- If you don't know the answer to a question, respond with "I don't know." In doing so, you will communicate a sense of honesty and a willingness to get down on your child's level.

In Conclusion

As children grow into adolescence, many times communication with parents becomes more complex. In my forty-four years as an educator, a number of parents expressed to me that communication was easier when their adolescent was younger. Although this may be true in some cases, adults must never use this as an excuse not to reach out to their adolescents in their grief.

The adult will be more helpful if they enter into the feelings of the adolescent without having a need to change those feelings. Feelings are hard to change and trying to change them will only prove frustrating. Also, the adolescent may see the attempt to change their feelings as a threat.

It is important to also realize that an adolescent's thought processes are different from adults. It is helpful for the adult to remember how they were as an adolescent to better see things from the adolescent's perspective.

The goals need to be helping the adolescent embrace fond memories of the person who died and helping them discover hope for their "new normal." Helping the adolescent work toward healing is a challenging task for the adult. But it is a task well worth taking. If the adolescent does not have the opportunity to speak with an adult who has more life experiences, their confusion may persist and their grief may go underground. The underground grief usually causes a great deal of emotional damage. Most times when the grief resurfaces, it is a common probability that a great deal of emotional damage has occurred.

Although many adolescents seem to be closer to their friends, grieving adolescents need adults to assist them through the grief process. Also, most times the adult needs to take the first step.

A Student's Story

A few years ago, I was facilitating an adolescent grief support group in a high school where I was an at-risk counselor. One of the group participants was a boy whose sister recently had died in a car accident. This boy was classified as "special needs" and had a reputation for acting out in his academic classes. Before each meeting, he would get out of class early to help me set up the room, then he would stay after the meetings to help me put the room back in place. One day after our meeting ended, he was helping me fold up chairs and said, "You want to know what I really like about our group meetings?" (I thought he was going to tell me he liked getting out of class early.) "We don't tell each other how to feel," he said. The point is: people are going to feel what they feel. Feelings aren't right or wrong; they just are. Our job as caring adults is to help adolescents appropriately express their feelings in a safe and caring atmosphere, not tell them what to and not to feel.

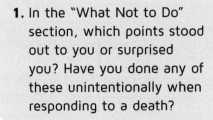

1. In the "What Not to Do" section, which points stood out to you or surprised you? Have you done any of these unintentionally when responding to a death?

2. In your experience, have you ever witnessed a student using any of the following coping techniques: cloning, overachieving, or isolation? Moving forward, what things can you say or do to help them?

3. In what ways can we encourage adolescent students experiencing grief?

KEY POINTS

- Most deaths that adolescents experience are sudden or untimely deaths. Many students will react with feelings of disbelief and numbness.

- After a tragedy affecting the school family, students should not be asked to continue with schoolwork as if nothing happened. The work of grieving must take precedence if these students are to begin the healing process.

- Some of the general copying techniques for adolescents are cloning, overachieving, or isolating.

- It is important to remember that adolescents don't think like adults. We can help normalize their feelings, listen, and empathize with what they are going through.

4 Responding to a Death by Suicide

I have been called upon many times to help a school that experienced a suicide of a student or staff member. In the following chapter, I will share how I responded to this unique type of death. Hopefully you will never have to use it. But if you do, you will want to decide whether you use this only for the student's class or if you use it for the entire student body. And, of course, be sure to secure permission from the deceased's family before you announce the cause of death as suicide. My hope is that the following material will be of help to your school family.

To the Student Body

When you are addressing the student's class or the entire student body, here is a sample assembly script you can use to communicate honestly and effectively.

I have been asked to share some hard and sad news with you today about the death of _____. As many of you have heard, the cause of death is suicide. We have asked all students to be here because we are family and we want you to know you are not alone in your pain. We are here to help you and walk through this with you. Our purpose is to validate all your emotions.

We hope that this time of aftercare helps you process this difficult experience. I ask you to use your gifts and talents to be a good friend, son, or daughter. Treat people with love and respect them for who they are as a tribute to _____.

The facts as we know them are: _____ was found yesterday at _____.

This is indeed a sad day for all of us. A tragedy like this can trigger many different emotions in us. Some of you may feel anger, and that is completely normal. Many of us feel this way. It does not mean we are bad people. It is okay to be angry. What makes anger wrong is what we do with it or how we handle it. There are two ways we should NOT handle anger. The first is to cover it up by stuffing it deep within us and not talking about it. Stuffing anger often leads to bitterness, grudges, and eventually depression. The second way we should not handle our anger is to go off on people. Mishandled anger leaves a trail of relational destruction in its wake. I am sure that most of us in here agree that this only adds fire to our already raw emotional wounds caused by this incident. Please don't deny your anger and pretend it doesn't exist. Deal with it respectfully, expressing your feelings to someone else and letting them know what your needs are related to this incident.

Another emotion you may be feeling is sadness. Then, some of you may feel nothing and this may scare you. However, this simply means you may be in a state of numbness and shock, which is a natural body defense mechanism.

If you ever have suicidal thoughts, please know that many people in this room, students and staff, care about you and are willing to help you. If you have a friend who confides these feelings to you, bring them to a responsible adult immediately.

Whatever feelings you may have, please know that feelings are not right or wrong; they just are. Don't judge each other's response to this tragedy.

Even though you may not have known _____ well, this tragedy may trigger the pain of other losses you have had in your life. This same may be true for your classmates. Don't judge their reactions. You don't know what they have gone through in their own life.

If you ever had a conflict with _____, forgive yourself. Many times, people have issues with other people. This is simply a part of being human and having relationships with others. It is extremely important to put this behind you.

Again, please don't spread rumors. Instead, spread understanding and respect. This will honor _____'s life. Let us make a corporate promise together in this room right now that this is going to be the last suicide at _____ School. Let us solidify this promise by raising our right hand now. Please keep your hand up and please look around the room.

Your teachers, counselors, principals, office staff, aids, cafeteria workers, custodians, and every adult staff member are all hurting because of this tragedy. They hurt because they care about _____'s family, and they also hurt because they know you are hurting and they care about you.

This type of tragedy stops here. We will commit to each other that we will share when we are hurting. We will care for each other and reach out to each other. We will get through this together.

Don't Forget the Staff

As you are speaking to the students in this assembly, you may wish to add the following:

Please know that the adults in our school who work with you are here because they care. They are dedicated to making positive difference in your lives. They are here to listen and comfort you as you all work through this tragedy. However, you must realize that your staff are people too. They have feelings and emotions and they need comfort and encouragement as well. Please consider giving one or more staff members a hug, side hug, handshake, or a word of appreciation. It is important that we all support each other and care for each other as we work through this tragedy.

Dismissal to Classrooms

After the assembly, I have found that the best practice is to send students and teachers back to their classrooms so they can further share feelings and discuss how to support each other. Both students and teachers tend to be more apt to share in a classroom setting than at a student assembly.

Discussion Guidelines for Classroom Teachers

The following guidelines should be given in writing to the classroom teachers facilitating the class discussion:

When Discussing Suicide with Your Class . . .

- Encourage students to express their feelings.
- Try not to let the discussion glamorize the act.
- Remind the students that no one is responsible.
- Reinforce that suicide is a tragedy.
- Do not allow someone to become bigger in death than they were in life.
- Remind students that there are many people at school and in the community who truly care about them.

Possible Discussion Questions

The teacher may choose some or all of the following questions depending on the unique situation of the tragedy:

- What thoughts and feelings might be involved in someone wanting to die by suicide?
- What might cause a person to have such thoughts and feelings?
- What must it be like for someone to have these thoughts and feelings?
- What possible reason might a person have for killing him/herself?
- What might a friend or classmate do for a friend who is having suicidal thoughts?
- Do you find yourself thinking and feeling differently about suicide now than when we first started talking about this?

These questions are only suggestions. Often, the classroom teacher knows her students and what questions will and will not work well with them. The teacher should take notice of any students who seem overly troubled or quiet and follow school protocol in getting them to the counseling center.

What to Do When a Student Talks to You About Suicide

Listen – Encourage the student to talk to you or some other trusted adult. Don't give advice or feel obligated to find simple solutions.

Be Honest – If you don't know what to say, say so. Don't be a cheerful phony. Students at **this age** know when you aren't being honest.

Share Feelings – At times, everyone feels sad, hurt, or hopeless. You know what that's like, so share your feelings with students. This will help them know that you are a person too and that they are not alone.

Get Help – Follow the school protocol. Professional help is crucial when something as serious as suicide is considered. Make sure you are fully informed of the school protocol.

Helping Parents Talk to Adolescents About Suicide

As you begin to talk with your child, try to refrain from attempting to problem-solve or minimize typical adolescent problems. These problems may not seem important to you, but they may seem very serious to the adolescent. The following are a few suggestions when one of your child's friends dies from suicide:

- Stay calm and listen. If your child becomes agitated, stay calm.

- Try not to become emotional. Just listen.

- Validate their feelings. You don't know how your child feels. You can only imagine.

- Stress that suicide is never a valid option. And tell them that as long as you are alive and able, you will be available to help them if they or someone they know is suicidal.

- Don't be judgmental by saying things like, "That issue is not worthy of being suicidal," "It's crazy to feel suicidal over something so trivial," "If he had better values, he wouldn't have done this," and so on.

- Help your child know and feel you will always be available to listen.

- Encourage your child to come to you if they have a friend talking about suicide.

Helping Parents Talk to Young Children About Suicide

Most of our attention in this chapter has focused on addressing suicide with adolescents. Before we close this important chapter, I want to take a moment to talk about how to address suicide with a much younger child. First, it is important for the parent to talk to the child as soon as possible. Sooner or later (often sooner), the child will find out. If the child finds out through someone other than you telling them, you risk a greater chance of fear and distrust from the child.

Start by sitting close to the child. You might hold their hand to help them feel safe. Then you can tell them, "I have something very sad to tell you. Talking about sad things may make us cry and that's okay." When you discuss the suicide, use the word "died." Then answer the child's questions as simply as possible, but don't give too much detail.

If the child asks what suicide is, explain that "suicide is when people die in a way where they do it to themselves. Many times, when people take their own lives, their minds are not thinking clearly. It is hard to understand, and it has nothing to do with you or me. You and I didn't do anything to cause this. People who die by suicide are not thinking right because their minds aren't thinking right."

If the child asks how he did it, spare the graphic details. Answer only the direct question. Don't give more details than what was asked. Use age appropriate language and explanations.

Hug your child, tell them you love them, and let them know you will always be willing to listen if they need to talk about it more.

In Conclusion

Following the suicide of a student or staff member, it is of the utmost importance for the school to respond honestly and as quickly as possible. Upon being informed of the suicide, the school family liaison should contact the family of the deceased to gain permission to address the incident at school as a suicide. I can't stress enough how important this is.

If possible, a staff meeting needs to take place before students come to school. A presentation of the facts should be given to all staff to prevent any harmful rumors. It is important for the staff to process the shock before they have to face students. In my profession, we call this "putting on your oxygen mask before assisting others." The staff should be informed of the revised schedule for the day and what is expected of them. The structure of the day could be followed as laid out in this chapter.

In my experience, I have worked with several schools who have had a suicidal tragedy; however, I wish to point to four such experiences where I had to prove the point that it is important for schools to address the issue and to do so promptly:

- A high school of about 1,200 students had eight student suicides in one year.
- Another high school had twelve student suicides in a year and a half.
- A middle school had three suicides in one month.
- A high school had three suicides and two serious attempts in one month.

When I was called to these schools to help, one of the most important things I did was to conduct research attempting to find some common cause(s). Although there were a number of possible common causes, the one factor in all of those situations was the failure of the school to quickly and honestly respond in a manner such as I have described in this chapter.

Many prevention experts will agree that one of the most important preventative strategies is to promote awareness of the suicide issue.[10] Holding the school assembly and having the classroom discussions will many times reveal other students and even staff members who are in a suicidal crisis. Although there are no surefire guarantees, the school's quick, compassionate, and honest response could help prevent further tragedies such as with the four schools I listed above.

A Student's Story

I recently worked with a high school that was reeling after a very popular student died by suicide. The tragedy rocked the entire school community. The administration responded appropriately by calling in a prevention specialist to conduct an entire school assembly. In the ensuing weeks, school staff detected a great deal of hurt and misery among the student body over this tragedy. I got a call from the school administration to come in and assess the severity of the situation. As I reviewed the school's procedure, I found there was no follow-up discussion after the assembly. The students were talked to, but they never had a chance to talk. The administration agreed to hold another school assembly with the opportunity for student discussions in group and classroom formats, using the structure suggested in this chapter. According to the school staff, healing began taking place soon after. Students were more open and leaning on each other for encouragement. The deceased student's close friends and many other students were learning that they may not ever get over this tragedy, but with each other, they could get through it. And this has been my experience in many other similar situations. Students need the opportunity to talk in a safe environment about a tragedy such as this, not just to be talked to. I applaud this school administration for being sensitive to the needs of their students.

QUESTIONS to CONSIDER

1. Has your school experienced a death by suicide? If so, what is your current protocol? And how do you address it with students?

2. What should you do if a student shares their (or a friend's) thoughts of suicide? What are the appropriate steps to take?

3. How can you best support parents in talking to their children about suicide?

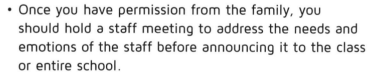

KEY POINTS

- It is extremely important to get permission from the deceased person's family before announcing a death by suicide to the school body.

- Once you have permission from the family, you should hold a staff meeting to address the needs and emotions of the staff before announcing it to the class or entire school.

- When addressing a death by suicide with the school body, share the facts and remind students that it is okay to feel many different emotions or even numbness. Remind them that they can talk to any teacher or adult if they are feeling similar thoughts of suicide.

- Responding honestly and quickly is key to preventing further cases of suicide in a school.

5

Forming a Support Group

Support groups offer a safe place for students to talk and tell their stories, which helps them process their grief in a healthy way and thus move forward. Providing students a safe place to share their feelings and hurts helps them find continued meaning in life and living. So, what should the goal of a support group be? Support groups should:

- Counter the sense of isolation by helping participants remember that they are not alone
- Provide emotional support in a non-judgmental atmosphere
- Help participants be kind and gentle to themselves and others
- Help participants provide support to other members of the group
- Help participants rediscover their zest for life

Getting Started

First, you need at least two students and no more than ten to start a support group. If you have more than ten students, separate the students into two groups by age or cause of death (suicide, sudden death, anticipated death, etc.). It is also important to have a co-facilitator. Two sets of adult eyes and experiences are helpful to recognize different grief reactions of the participants. If a student becomes overwhelmed, sad, or angry and walks out of the room, one of the adults can follow the student to assist them. This is a service to this student and limits any chance of liability. If the adult can't help the student normalize, it is recommended that they stay with the student or release them to a school administrator until the student can be released to a parent or other responsible adult.

Establish a Structure

To identify students who may benefit from a support group, the school counselor can send out an announcement to the teaching staff stating that they want to start a grief support group and asking them to refer students who have experienced a loss to them. Once there are students who agree to participate and they have a signed permission slip from their parents or guardians, the school counselor should identify and locate age-appropriate support materials that will be helpful. Then, they can determine the length and frequency of the meetings. The length of the meetings should be long enough for every participant to have a chance to share. When I would facilitate support groups, my group would meet during lunch hour so none of the students had to be pulled from class. Finding a meeting place is also an important aspect to the structure. The meeting place should be away from heavy traffic areas of the school, and, ideally, it should have a low ceiling and soft lighting to provide privacy and intimacy for the participants.

Support Group Ground Rules

Having and obeying simple ground rules is critical to the success of the group. I suggest you start each meeting with a quick review of the ground rules and have them posted in an area where all the participants can see them. Below is a sample list of ground rules:

1. No two people are alike. Respect and accept what you have in common with others and what is unique to you.

2. Please respect others' right to pass.

3. Make every effort not to interrupt when someone is speaking.

4. Turn cell phones off during meeting.

5. Do not use the names of fellow participants outside this room.

6. Attend each meeting and be on time.

7. It is okay to be angry, but we don't throw chairs, punch walls, or scream at others in this room. This is a safe place for all.

8. Confidentiality will be kept here, unless someone states harm to someone or to themselves.

I have found it very helpful to *quickly* repeat the ground rules at the start of every session. Please see Appendix 4 for the Support Group Statements of Beliefs.

Group Meeting Itinerary

The following group meeting itineraries are meant to help you make the most of your time with students. You can certainly choose your own activities or questions for each session.

Meeting One (Welcome, orientation, and goals for the group)

- Personal introductions – Allow students to go around the circle and share their name and grade.

- Go over the ground rules and the reasons for them.

- Participants should fill out the questions about their deceased loved one and get in groups of two to review the questions. (See Appendix 5.)

- Group members should fill out the "Thinking of You" Fact Sheet. (See Appendix 3.)

- As students share, stress to them that they are having normal reactions to an abnormal situation.
- It may be helpful to have a light snack and drinks as students are socializing.
- Remind students to bring a photo of their loved one to the next meeting.

"Thinking of You" Cards

The "Thinking of You" Fact Sheets, which should be handed out to each student during the first session, are for them to list specifically difficult days or anticipated difficult days that lie ahead. Examples of these days might be:

1. The deceased person's birthday
2. The anniversary of death
3. Mother's Day/Father's Day
4. Parents' wedding anniversary (if a parent died)
5. Any day they feel may be difficult for them (see Appendix 3)

On those dates, the facilitator may write a "Thinking of You" card for the student. This is not a sympathy card. Instead, it is a thoughtful note to the student saying that you care and remember the importance of this day. The card may have a comforting picture on the front with the words "Thinking of You." And the note can simply say, "I just want you to know that I care and am thinking of you today." For particularly difficult situations, it would be a nice touch to give every staff person in the school an opportunity to sign the card. Then, if possible, hand deliver it to the student on that specific day. During the summer months, you could place the letter in the mail if you can't personally deliver it. This will be very encouraging and uplifting to the student. In my adolescent support groups, once students started receiving some of these cards from adults, the students started making them on their own to give to fellow group participants.

Meeting Two (Students are reminded ahead of time to bring a photo of their friend or loved one to this session.)

- Quickly repeat the ground rules.
- Participants show photos and share why they picked that particular photo of their friend or loved one.
- Introduce the following discussion questions:
  - Are people treating you differently now than before your loss?
  - If so, how does that make you feel?
  - Has anyone (no names) minimized your grief? (Give examples of minimizing. For example, "at least" statements.)

Meeting Three

- Quickly repeat the ground rules.
- Continue the discussion on minimizing and explain that their friends are trying to be helpful. Ask, "How can you respond to people when they say something that is well-intended but inappropriate? Examples are: "It's been six months. You should be getting over it." "Once you start partying again, you will feel better." "I know how you feel."
- Encourage participants to be kind to themselves. Give examples of how they can do this.

  (Use positive self-talk, give themselves some slack, share a small act of kindness to a friend, parent, sibling, etc.)

Meeting Four (Examining common grief myths)

- Quickly repeat the ground rules.
- Draw attention to the display board listing common grief myths. (See Appendix 1.)
- As a group, discuss why these statements are myths.
- Discuss the importance of understanding basic facts about grief.

The remaining meetings for the group can be determined by the facilitators based on the unique needs of the group.

Beware of Red Flags

As group facilitators, you need to be aware of red flag behaviors that signal a need to make an appropriate referral for professional help. Examples of red flags are as follows:

- Expressions of suicidal thoughts or intent
- A pattern of substance abuse
- Inability to care for self (not sleeping, eating, etc.)
- Physical harm to self
- Uncontrollable phobias (for example, the inability to be by themselves at any time)
- Characteristics of grieving that do not appear to change over an extended period of time.

Important Things to Consider

It is a good practice to send a permission slip home to parents, briefly explaining the purpose of the group. Also, understand that most people are not ready for a support group for the first few months after the tragedy. The shock and numbness may need to wear off first before they are ready to participate in a group meeting.

It is also important to establish the duration of the group. Support groups that go on for too long can sometimes become a hindrance to healing. I have found in my experience that the duration should be determined by the group facilitators after about seven to eight sessions. If it is decided to end the group, you can give the participants at least three sessions' worth of notice before the meetings come to an end. I have had groups that met for ten sessions and groups that met for twenty sessions. This really depends on the needs and progress of the participants.

It is vitally important that the facilitators establish a caring, trusting relationship with each participant. It is also important to occasionally check in with each participant after the support group comes to an end. We should be committed to the continual growth and healing of the participants, and the participants should feel and see evidence of our care and concern. Please see Appendix 6 for an End of Support Group Evaluation.

In Conclusion

A grief support group is a valuable service to the grieving students in your school community in helping them to get to their "new normal." Along with assisting students through their individual grief process, I have found a special bonding takes place within the group. The sharing of their experiences and struggles helps them become more sensitive to each other and sheds light on better handling their own individual challenges. As educators, we desire to develop the whole child, which involves their hearts as well as their minds. A well-planned and well-run support group is a beneficial tool in getting the social-emotional development of your students back on track. My fellow co-facilitators and I have found these experiences most rewarding for us as well.

A Student's Story

Mary (not her real name), a student in my seventh-grade science class, lost her mother to cancer. It was a devastating experience for this young girl. She struggled with this tragedy all through high school and finally came to my adolescent grief support group her senior year. As the year progressed, I could see her making strides in getting a handle on her grief. As Mother's Day approached, along with her high school graduation, she sat talking with her friends in class. She told them that Mother's Day was a hard day for her, and on top of that, her mother wouldn't be at her coming graduation. Her math teacher overheard her and asked, "Mary, how long ago did your mother die?" Mary responded, "Five years ago." The teacher seemed taken back and said, "Five years ago? Girl, get over it." Mary was crushed. Fortunately, we had a grief group session that same day. Mary walked into the meeting in tears. She told the group what happened in her math class. My co-facilitator and I were very impressed and encouraged by the participants' responses. On Mother's Day, the group participants made a "Thinking of You" card for Mary. All the participants of the group who were underclassmen showed up at the graduation commencement to support her. This was done without any encouragement or directive from us. The students did this on their own. The point is, when we genuinely support those who grieve, they, in turn, will show support for each other. Grief shared is grief diminished. Many times, we comfort those with the comfort we received from others.

1. Does your school currently facilitate small groups for grieving students? If so, what do they look like and have they been successful?

2. If you do not currently have a support group in your school, what teachers or staff could you identify to help start one? And what time would best work during the school day?

3. Have you ever witnessed any of the red flag behaviors listed in this chapter in any of your students? If so, how might you reach out to these students to offer support and help?

KEY POINTS

- Support groups help students process their grief in a healthy way. They provide students with a safe place to share their grief and get emotional support from others.

- To start a support group, you should have at least two, but no more than ten, students in a group. If you have more than ten students, you can break the group into two smaller groups. Students should have a signed permission slip to be part of the group. And you should also have a co-facilitator present.

- At the first meeting, you should introduce the students to the Support Group Ground Rules, then at every other meeting, you should review them at the start of the meeting.

- It is important for you to watch for red flag behaviors that signal when a student may need to be referred to a professional.

Conclusion

Throughout an educator's career, there will be many students in the school or classroom who are grieving over a significant loss. Many educators feel frustrated, not knowing what to do when confronted with a grieving student. The natural tendency is to give the problem to the school counselor. However, in most cases, counseling is not the most urgent need. The most urgent need of the grieving student is for comfort. Unless their need for comfort is met, students can experience a temporary cognition deficit. They will struggle to "connect the dots." But comfort brings regulation and helps the cognition process of the student.

An adult doesn't need a counseling degree to comfort and listen. When a tragedy happens in the school community, it should be a school family issue, not just a counseling department issue. Students should be afforded the opportunity to seek out and talk to any caring adult staff member of their choosing. After regulation takes place, counseling will likely be a more helpful experience.

As I travel the country presenting training for the tragedy component of school crisis teams, a few teachers have said to me, "This is not what I signed up for when I decided to be a teacher." I kindly remind them that we aren't only responsible for students' academic development, but for their social-emotional development as well. We teach children and adolescents more than just subject matter. Death is a part of life, and when our students experience loss, we need to demonstrate compassion and caring for them. This is a critically valuable lesson for all of us.

Another question I occasionally get is, "Isn't this the job of the parents?" My response is yes; it is the parents' job. However, many loving parents need and want our help in dealing with their grieving child or adolescent. And unfortunate as it is, for many students, when it comes to family, school is as good as it gets. We must stand in as their family.

I strongly believe that with some training, classroom teachers can discuss and defuse, helping the school counselor to counsel in a more effective and productive manner.

As educators, I feel we have the awesome responsibility of working with the most precious resource our country has—its children. We have the opportunity to make a positive difference in the lives of our students. Hard times come to make us better, not bitter. The longer we work in education, the more positive influence, encouragement, and hope we can impart to these precious resources. We cannot fix a tragedy, but we can help instill hope in the students in our school family.

APPENDIX

Grief Myths and Facts

MYTHS	FACTS
The pain will go away if you ignore it.	Acknowledging the pain is best. If we don't hurt, we won't heal.
If we don't cry, we aren't grieving.	Crying isn't the only response to grief.
Time will heal.	It is what we do with time that heals.
Grieving is dysfunctional.	NOT grieving a loss is dysfunctional.
I must protect my child from such pain.	I must help attend to my child's pain.
Grief is a mental illness.	Grief is a normal response to loss.
People go through predictable stages.	Grief is an individual unique journey.
It's okay to "fudge" a few facts to my child.	Honesty is the best policy.
With time, we can get back to "normal."	There now will be a new "normal."
My pain is due to a lack of faith.	People of faith also grieve.
I have to be strong for my child.	It is okay to let the child know you are grieving too.
I don't feel anything. Something is wrong.	Usually, numbness sets in at first.
A child's grief is short in duration.	A child's grief may be long, possibly longer than many adults.
I can help my child get over her grief.	Grief is an experience you never get over, but you can get through.

Normal Versus Abnormal Grief for Children and Adolescents

NORMAL	ABNORMAL
Responds to comfort and support	Rejects comfort and support
Uses play to express grief	Resists play
Connects depressed feelings with death	Doesn't relate feeling to life events
Often open and angry	May not directly express anger
Still experiences moments of joy	Projects a pervasive sense of doom
Caring adults can sense a feeling of chronic sadness and emptiness	Projects hopelessness and emptiness
May express guilt over some aspect	Has overwhelming feelings of guilt about the loss
Self-esteem temporarily impacted	Deep loss of self-esteem

Grief Support Group
"Thinking of You" Fact Sheet

_____

YOUR NAME

_____

NAME OF DECEASED

_____

DATE OF DEATH

☐ Parent   ☐ Sibling
☐ Grandparent   ☐ Godparent
☐ Close Friend   ☐ Aunt/Uncle
☐ Significant Person

_____

DECEASED'S BIRTHDAY

_____

PARENTS' WEDDING ANNIVERSARY

_____

YOUR BIRTHDAY

Days that are especially difficult for you:

_____

_____

_____

Support Group
Statement of Beliefs

1. We understand that grief is a unique experience to every individual.

2. We will respect each other's differences and also what is unique to you.

3. We won't set a timetable on how long it should take you or others to heal.

4. We do respect a person's preference to listen without sharing during our meetings.

5. We will make every effort not to interrupt when someone is sharing with the group.

6. We will respect all members' right to confidentially.

7. We will not use names of fellow participants in discussions outside our group.

8. We believe that the only advice given should be asked for by a participant.

9. The group facilitators believe each person should have equal time to express their feelings.

10. The group facilitators believe that no one or few persons should monopolize group time.

11. The group facilitators are committed to creating an atmosphere of calm, trust, and sharing of feelings in a safe environment.

Grief Support Group
Session One Participant Discussion Format

1. Give a handout to each participant and have them fill out the following information about their deceased loved one:

    1. This person was my _____.

    2. The thing I liked best about my _____ is

       _____.

    3. The thing I miss most about my _____ is

       _____.

    4. When I feel sad and lonely without my

       _____ I can _____.

    5. When I want to talk about my _____ I

       can _____.

2. Place participants in groups of two.

3. Participants will share with a partner what they wrote in the blanks. Facilitator should then ask for participants to share with the entire group.

I have found this activity very valuable in breaking the ice and opening the door for deeper sharing in the following group sessions.

End of Support Group Evaluation

At the end of the last meeting, the group facilitators should hand out a survey to assess how the group's sessions helped the participants in their grief journey and how they may be able to enhance the quality of future groups. The following is a list of items that may prove to be helpful:

1. Participant Name_____ (optional)

2. The support group meetings helped me.
   ☐ strongly agree
   ☐ agree
   ☐ disagree

3. Our support group meetings helped me better understand my grief process.
   ☐ strongly agree
   ☐ agree
   ☐ disagree

4. Our support group meetings helped me understand the unique grief processes of others.
   ☐ strongly agree
   ☐ agree
   ☐ disagree

5. I feel comfortable that the things I shared in the group will remain confidential.
   ☐ strongly agree
   ☐ agree
   ☐ disagree

6. The group facilitators did a good job of running the meetings.
   ☐ strongly agree
   ☐ agree
   ☐ disagree

7. Please share any thoughts you have about making a future grief support group more helpful to the participants:

_____

_____

_____

DOWNLOADABLE RESOURCES

The resources in this book are available for you
as a digital download!

Please visit **15minutefocusseries.com** and click this book
cover on the page. Once you've clicked the book cover,
a prompt will ask you for a code to unlock the activities.

Please enter code:

Grief320

References

David A. Opalewski and Joel C. Robertson, *Confronting Death in the School Family*, Revised Edition, (Chattanooga: The National Center for Youth Issues, 2017).

David A. Opalewski and John Belaski, *Understanding and Addressing Children's Grief Issues* (Chattanooga: The National Center for Youth Issues, 2008).

David A. Opalewski and Joel Robertson, *Understanding and Addressing Adolescent Grief Issues* (Chattanooga: The National Center for Youth Issues, 2010).

Dr. David A. Opalewski, "Weathering the Storm," *Student Assistance Journal*, Fall 2005.

Patrick O'Malley, *Getting Grief Right* (Sounds True Publishing, 2017).

Erica Goldblatt Hyatt, DSW, *Grieving the Sibling You Lost* (Instant Help Books, 2015).

Marc Gellman, *And God Cried, Too: A Kid's Book of Healing and Hope* (New York: Harper-Trophy, 2002).

Elinor Lipman, "Finding the Right Words," *Good Housekeeping Magazine*, December 2010.

Alan Wolfelt, *Healing the Bereaved Child* (Routledge, 1996).

Susanne Bauer, "'Do You Like Your Therapist's Voice?': The Relevance of Tone of Voice in Psychotherapy," *Voices Resources*, March 2010.

Taryn Davies, "The Importance of Tone of Voice and Why We Should Get It Right," *Pixus*, March 3, 2015.

Notes

1 William Steele and Caelan Kuban, "Advancing Trauma-Informed Practices," The National Institute for Trauma and Loss in Children, 2016, https://starr.org/wp-content/uploads/TLC-Whitepaper.pdf.

2 David A. Opalewski and Joel C. Robertson, *Confronting Death in the School Family*, Revised Edition, (Chattanooga: The National Center for Youth Issues, 2017).

3 Elinor Lipman, "Finding the Right Words," *Good Housekeeping Magazine*, December 2010.

4 "What Is Cortisol?" WebMD, https://www.webmd.com/a-to-z-guides/what-is-cortisol#1.

5 Granger Westberg, *Good Grief: A Companion for Every Loss* (Fortress Press, 1970).

6 Susanne Bauer, "'Do You Like Your Therapist's Voice?': The Relevance of Tone of Voice in Psychotherapy," *Voices Resources*, March 2010.

7 Alan Wolfelt, *Healing the Bereaved Child* (Routledge, 1996).

8 Catherine H. Rogers, Frank J. Floyd, Marshal Mailick Seltzer, Jan Greenberg, and Jinkuk Hong, "Long-term Effects of the Death of a Child on Parents' Adjustment in Midlife," J Fam Psychol 2008 April; 22(2): 203–211.

9 Taryn Davies, "The Importance of Tone of Voice and Why We Should Get It Right," *Pixus*, March 3, 2015.

10 The Michigan Association of Suicidology, MI State Conference, 1997 Statement of Belief.

About the Author

David Opalewski, M.A. is the founder and president of Grief Recovery, Inc., in Saginaw, Michigan, a consultant and author of *Confronting Death in the School Family, Understanding and Addressing Adolescent Grief Issues, Understanding and Addressing Children's Grief Issues*, and *Answering the Cry for Help: Suicide Prevention and Intervention for Schools and Communities*.

David has a forty-four-year career in education. He has taught at the elementary, middle, high school, and college levels and was an at-risk counselor for eight of those years. He retired from Central Michigan University in May of 2017 as Professor Emeritus.

During Opalewski's educational career, he experienced the combined deaths of twenty-six students and fellow staff members. He was a replacement teacher in a fifth-grade classroom for a teacher who was killed in an auto accident during the middle of the school year.

David worked part time for three years in a funeral home as an aftercare consultant to the families of the deceased. In 1989 he married a former widow and adopted her two boys, ages seven and five. These experiences were major learning experiences for him in the areas of grief and bereavement.

He is a widely sought-after conference speaker and trainer for the tragedy component of school crisis teams across the country.

David can be reached at **griefrecoveryinc@gmail.com** or you can visit his website at **www.griefrecovery.ws**.

Other books from David Opalewski

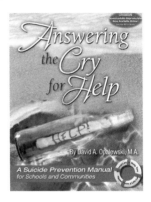

Answering the Cry for Help: A Suicide Prevention Manual for Schools and Counselors   (Gr K-12)

Provides guidelines for developing a Community Suicide Prevention Program that promotes awareness about risks. Discusses methods for suicide prevention, establishes guidelines and resources for intervention and seeks to educate and train Crisis Team members and community leaders to manage possible situations and scenarios.

Confronting Death in the School Family   (Gr K-12)

Guidelines and tools to help your crisis response team respond to the death of a student or staff member. Includes procedures for response, sample announcements, comprehensive classroom plans, and worksheets for parents and teachers. A suicide prevention curriculum is also included.

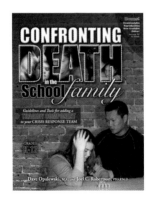

Understanding and Addressing Children's Grief Issues   (Gr PK-5)

Children who have experienced grief are at a higher risk for depression as they grow. This informative workbook will provide you with comprehensive techniques to address the situation.

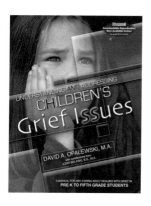

Understanding and Addressing Adolescent Grief Issues   (Gr 6-12)

A guide for helping adolescents through the troubling times caused by a death experience. Helps you understand what the adolescent is going through and gives you comprehensive techniques to address the situation and help foster growth and maturity.